Faith Parenting Guide
Camels Don't Fly

Cooperation: I want to help my child learn to work together with others to accomplish goals.

Sound: Read the story of *Camels Don't Fly* with your child. Talk about a time when you or your child wanted to do something special but you weren't sure how to do it. Let's say you wanted to learn to ride a bike. Was it hard to do? Did you need help? Did you ever fall? Did you keep trying? Honk, the camel, is just like that. He wants to try to do something that he doesn't know how to do without some help.

Sight: Look at the drawings of the animals in Noah's Park. Discuss the setting. Why were the animals there? What were they trying to do? How did they try to understand the ways of God?

Touch: Write your own story or make a picture of something that was hard or new for you to do. Show it to your family and talk about how much it helps when you all pitch in together to get something done. Read the real story of Noah in Genesis 6–9 in your favorite Bible.

Honk stopped at the brook to look at
himself in a pool of calm water.
His coat glistened in the sun,
and his bright, white teeth
gleamed. He was one
good-looking camel,
he thought
to himself.

Noah's Park

CAMELS DON'T FLY

Written by Richard Hays
Illustrated by Chris Sharp

Faith Kids

an imprint of Cook Communications, Colorado Springs, Colorado 80918
Cook Communications, Paris, Ontario
Kingsway Communications, Eastbourne, England

CAMELS DON'T FLY
©1999 by The Illustrated Word, Inc.

First printing, 1999
Printed in Canada
03 02 01 00   5 4 3 2

Digital art and design: Gary Currant
Executive Producer: Kenneth R. Wilcox

Library of Congress Cataloging-in-Publication Data

Hays, Richard.
   Camels Don't Fly / written by Richard Hays ; illustrated by Chris Sharp.
      p. cm. -- (Noah's Park)
   Summary: After several unsuccessful attempts to fly, Honk the camel comes to appreciate
the gifts God has given him.
   ISBN 0-7814-3350-9
   [1. Camels Fiction. 2. Flight Fiction. 3. Self-acceptance -Religious aspects Fiction. 4. Animals
Fiction.] I. Sharp, Chris, 1954- ill. II. Title, III. Hays, Richard. Noah's Park.
PZ7.H314924Cam 1999
[E]--dc21   99-39079
                                                           CIP

The pleased camel smiled, but then frowned. Was that a spot of dirt just below his large, handsome nose? Honk hated being dirty. Dirt spoiled his natural good looks. He lowered his head to the water to take a closer look just as something dropped from the sky, banged him on the head, and splashed water all over his face.

Honk looked up and saw Shadow, the raccoon, drop from a limb of an overhanging palm tree and then scamper away. The soggy camel honked loudly at the pesky raccoon.

The camel honked when he was mad, honked when he was sad, and even honked when he was happy. That's why everyone just called him Honk.

Honk looked down and saw the coconut lying in the water. He pushed at it with his nose, and it rolled away.
The camel honked loudly to himself.
There was something shiny hidden in the water.

Honk carefully dug up the object
and pulled it onto the sand.
When he saw what it was,
he jumped away in surprise.
It was a statue of a camel. In fact,
the statue looked very much like
Honk himself, but this camel
had wings!

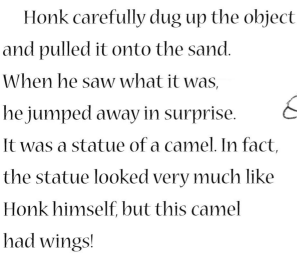

Honk was amazed. He had always
dreamed of flying. He often imagined
himself soaring to the clouds
and talking to the birds
as they flew alongside him.
He liked birds.
They all seemed
to be very clean.

Where had the statue come from?
wondered Honk. He didn't know, but his friend,
Ponder the frog, probably would. Honk held up the statue
and asked, "Does this mean that camels can fly?"
Then the camel hurried off to find Ponder
and his other friends.

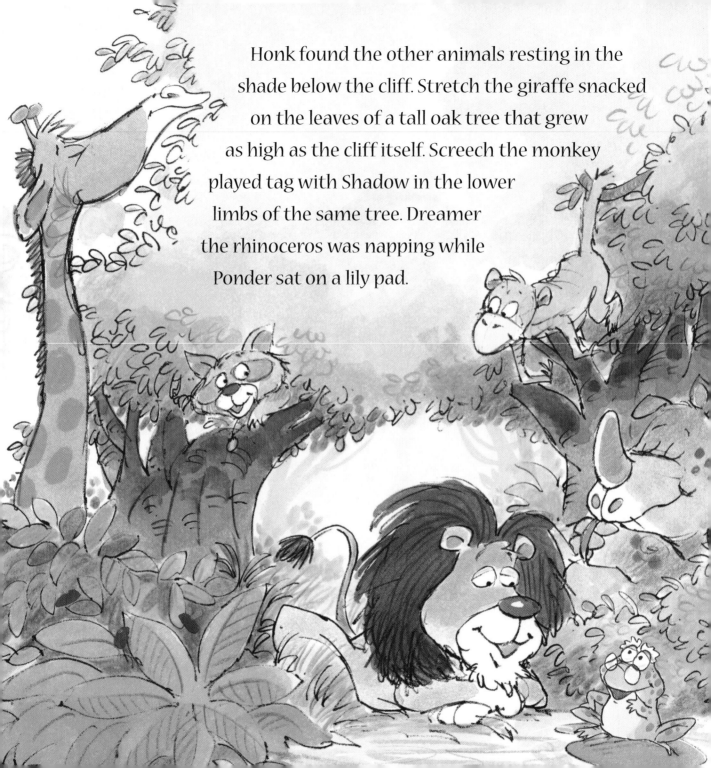

Honk found the other animals resting in the shade below the cliff. Stretch the giraffe snacked on the leaves of a tall oak tree that grew as high as the cliff itself. Screech the monkey played tag with Shadow in the lower limbs of the same tree. Dreamer the rhinoceros was napping while Ponder sat on a lily pad.

The frog was talking to Howler the lion.

"Look! Look everyone at what I've found!" The excited camel rushed around showing each of the animals his wonderful discovery. Honk believed that the statue proved that camels could indeed fly. They just needed wings!

Stretch bent down to see
what the camel was so excited
about. Shadow and Screech
tried to look, too,
but instead fell from
their limbs right on top
of Howler.

The lion roared, sending Shadow and Screech back up the tree.

"I've found proof that camels can fly,"
Honk wheezed, a little out of breath.
"This camel has wings. If I had wings,
I could fly, too!"

Shadow and Screech
looked at the camel
and fell from the tree again.
This time they hit the
ground and rolled
around.
They flapped
their arms
and laughed
at the camel.

"Honk," said Ponder gently, "camels don't fly. God has blessed each of us with unique gifts and talents. I can hop and swim, Stretch can reach high in the trees to find food, Screech can swing from his tail, and you, Honk, can walk a great distance without needing water. It is important for us to remember how special each of our gifts is and to be thankful to God for them. I'm sorry, Honk, but camels don't fly."

Honk was clearly not satisfied.

"This shows that camels *can* fly." Honk shook the statue
at the others. "Someone must have seen a camel flying
if they made this statue. Maybe I lost my wings after the flood.
What if I am supposed to fly but just don't know it?

Now I am going to make some wings, and then you will see a camel fly." Ponder shook his head. How would Noah have handled this? he wondered. Noah would pray to God for the answer, Ponder suddenly realized. The wise frog nodded to himself and decided to say a prayer for Honk. He had a feeling the camel would need it.

The next day, Honk came back into the clearing. He wore a harness of vines over his humps. Attached to the harness was a pair of stiff wooden wings that stood straight out from the camel's side. Ponder, Shadow, and a few others watched as Honk climbed to the top of the cliff and ran as fast as he could over the edge.

For a moment, the camel
seemed to hover in the air.
Then he crashed into the
water with a big splash.

Honk swam over to the edge
and climbed out of the water.
He blew a great spout
of water from his nose.
"Wings are too stiff,"
he sputtered,
and then
walked away.

The next day, everyone watched very closely as Honk again climbed to the top of the cliff. This time he wore wings made from palm leaves.

Honk raced to the edge and once more
jumped off. He flapped with all his strength,
but the wings were too delicate. Again he
crashed into the water. "Too weak,"
he told the others this time.

Each day for the next two weeks Honk tried to fly.
He tried wings made from small leaves and
wings made from grass. He tried
wings made from walnut shells
and wings made from bamboo.
He even tried to get feathers from Flutter,
but the dove was too small to give up that many feathers.

Finally, after many failures, the bruised camel sat down to talk to Ponder.

"I know what you're going to say," Honk said to the frog. "Camels don't fly!"

"Let me ask you a question," Ponder said. "Have you learned anything at all in the past few days?"

"I have learned that trying to fly hurts!" Honk said sheepishly. "And I have also learned that I like being the way I am. None of the other animals try to be something they aren't. I just thought it would be fun to fly once."

"Honk, you have learned that you are special just the way you are. You are precious in God's sight whether you fly, walk, run, or crawl. Because of that, tomorrow your friends are going to help you make your dream come true."

The next day all the
animals gathered once
more. At the top of the
cliff Honk stood, wearing
wings made from the feathers
of hundreds of birds that
Flutter had called to help.
Each bird had given two
feathers to make the wings.

Besides the wings, there
were dozens, perhaps
hundreds, of vines tied to Honk's legs
and body. At the other end of each
vine was one of the
birds that had gathered
for the event.

On Ponder's signal
all the birds flapped
their wings, and Honk,
flapping his own wings,
jumped from the cliff.
All of the other animals
watched as the camel
first fell, then slowly
rose into the air.

For the first time and probably
last time, a camel flew.

Honk had realized his dream!

Everyone cheered, and Ponder thanked
God for the answer to his prayer to help Honk fly.
He knew God would continue to bless all the animals just
as He had blessed Noah all those years ago.

Noah's Park™ MAP

Nosy Rock

Screech's Hollow

Cozy Cave

Polka-Dot Pond

DREAMER HAS A NIGHTMARE

Dreamer the rhinoceros loves to dream, until one day he has his first nightmare. How will Dreamer handle this frightening experience? Discover the answer in the Noah's Park adventure, Dreamer Has a Nightmare.

STRETCH'S TREASURE HUNT

Stretch the giraffe grew up watching her parents search for the Treasure of Nosy Rock. Imagine what happens when she finds out that the treasure might be buried in Noah's Park. Watch the fur fly as Stretch and her friends look for treasure in Stretch's Treasure Hunt.